Let's Get Ready for Thanksgiving

By Joanne Winne

Welcome Books

Children's Press
A Division of Scholastic Inc.
New York / Toronto / London / Auckland / Sydney
Mexico City / New Delhi / Hong Kong
Danbury, Connecticut

Photo Credits: Cover and all photos by Maura Boruchow
Contributing Editors: Jeri Cipriano, Jennifer Silate
Book Design: Michelle Innes

Visit Children's Press on the Internet at:
http://publishing.grolier.com

Library of Congress Cataloging-in-Publication Data

Winne, Joanne.
   Let's get ready for Thanksgiving / by Joanne Winne.
   p. cm. — (Celebrations)
   Includes index.
   ISBN 0-516-23176-6 (lib. bdg.) — ISBN 0-516-29572-1 (pbk.)
   1. Thanksgiving Day—Juvenile literature. [1. Thanksgiving Day. 2. Holidays.] I. Title.
   II. Celebrations (Children's Press)
   GT4975 .W55 2001
   394.2649—dc21

                                                          00-047536

J
394.2649
W

Contents

Look at the **calendar**.

Today is Thanksgiving.

5

Thanksgiving began a long time ago.

It began when the **Pilgrims** first came to America.

7

The Pilgrims did not have much food when they came to America.

They were cold and hungry.

Native Americans helped the Pilgrims.

Native Americans and the Pilgrims shared food.

They **celebrated** the first Thanksgiving together.

We are making food for Thanksgiving.

We will share it with others, too.

13

I help to set the table and fold the napkins.

Family and friends come.

They also bring food
to share.

We are **thankful** for our family and friends.

19

We share our
Thanksgiving dinner.

New Words

calendar (**kal**-uhn-duhr) a chart showing the months, weeks, and days of the year

celebrated (**sehl**-uh-brayt-uhd) having had a party or an activity on a special day

Native Americans (**nay**-tihv uh-**mer**-uh-kuhnz) the first people to live in America

Pilgrims (**pihl**-gruhmz) English settlers who came to America

thankful (**thangk**-fuhl) feeling pleased or grateful about something

To Find Out More

Books
The Thanksgiving Story
by Alice Dalgliesh
Simon & Schuster Children's

Today Is Thanksgiving!
by Patrick K. Hallinan
Hambleton-Hill Publishing

Web Site
Kid's Domain Thanksgiving
http://www.kidsdomain.com/holiday/thanks/index.html
This Web site has a lot of fun Thanksgiving activities and stories.

Index

About the Author

Joanne Winne taught fourth grade for nine years. She currently writes and edits books for children. She lives in Hoboken, New Jersey.

Reading Consultants

Kris Flynn, Coordinator, Small School District Literacy, The San Diego County Office of Education

Shelly Forys, Certified Reading Recovery Specialist, W.J. Zahnow Elementary School, Waterloo, IL

Sue McAdams, Certified Reading Recovery Specialist and Literary Consultant, Dallas, TX